Bridges to Intimacy

C. Jesse Carlock

AND

Patricia T. Hagerty

LP LEARNING PUBLICATIONS, INC.
Holmes Beach, FL   Montreal

ISBN 1-55691-037-1

© 1991 by C. Jesse Carlock and Patricia Hagerty

All rights reserved. No part of this book may be reproduced or transmitted in any form or by any means, electronic or mechanical, including photocopying and recording, or by any information or retrieval systems, without permission in writing from the publisher.

Learning Publications, Inc.
5351 Gulf Drive
P.O. Box 1338
Holmes Beach, FL 34218-1338

Printing: 6 5 4 3 2   Year: 7 6 5 4 3

Printed in the United States of America.

We dedicate this book to Virginia Satir and Bunny Duhl for their guidance, inspiration, and loving encouragement.

TABLE OF CONTENTS

LIST OF FIGURES v
FOREWORD vii
PREFACE ix
PART A: PARTNERS: AN INTRODUCTION 1
PART B: OUR FAMILIES OF ORIGIN 5

Exercises

 1. Roots - Family of Origin Maps 7
 2. Photographs: "Hey, Look Me Over" 15
 3. Looking Back 17
 4. Relationship Path 21
 5. Relationship Metaphors 25
 6. Memories 27
 7. The Interpersonal Vulnerability Contract 29

PART C: OUR CONTACTS WITH EACH OTHER 35

Exercises

 8. Interpersonality Contact Survey 37
 9. Seeing 43
10. Attending to the Inner Voice 45
11. Touching 47
12. Boundaries: Values 49
13. Body Boundaries 51
14. Space and Time Boundaries 53
15. Interest Boundaries 57
16. Differences 59
17. Blaming and Defending 63
18. The Stress Ballet 65
19. Toy Defense 67

PART D: OUR STRENGTHS 71

Exercises

20. Wheel of Support 73
21. Relationship Glue 75
22. Famous Figures 77
23. Sharing Your Love 79
24. What I Like About You and Me 81

PART E: MAINTAINING OUR RELATIONSHIPS 85

Exercises

25. Taking the Temperature of the Relationship 87
26. Connect-O-Meter 89
27. Getting Your Needs Met 91
28. Make a Wish 93
29. Intimacy Request 95
30. Monthly Mystery 97

BIBLIOGRAPHY 99

LIST OF FIGURES

Figure Number		Page
1	Family of Origin	8
2	Maternal Grandparents	9
3	Paternal Grandparents	10
4	Our Relationship Path	22
5	Wheel of Support	74
6	Relationship Glue	75
7	Temperature Reading	88

FOREWORD

Discovering that one is an adult child of a dysfunctional family can be quite a shock. More importantly it is an extremely important step in healing. However, knowing how one was hindered in growing up is not enough. For unless we learn new ways of feeling and interacting, we continue the patterns we have learned.

Jesse Carlock and Patricia Hagerty know this very well. For many years they have helped adults learn new ways of relating to others, ways that are respectful and empowering. They know only too well that when one's sense of self-esteem is low, one tends to choose a partner who hopefully, by his or her mere presence, will raise that level of self-esteem. Paradoxically, many choose others who possess and exhibit patterns, both positive and negative, which are familiar. And so, the old family dances of dysfunction tend to continue. Partners still do not feel worthy or good about themselves, though they might feel good about having the other person.

Fortunately, there are now many programs which help adults who were children in dysfunctional families; who were children in families where they failed to grow up feeling good and confident about themselves. However, there are not many places or materials which are geared to helping adults learn new ways to partner, to become close, to be intimate, which focus on both persons at the same time.

This workbook fills that need. The authors have drawn from a wide range of resources and models and culled an extraordinary selection of exercises. These are exercises which partners can do in the privacy of their homes, or in groups with others, should they so choose. Couples may pick from the various categories those exercises which fit them at different moments in their relationship, and discover not only each other, but new ways to feel and think about each other, themselves and their relationship. Some exercises require more thought, others more a sense of play. Some dig into the past, others stay with the present, and still others push into the future. There is something here to fit the preferences of individual personal styles. And best of all, partners have the freedom to be in charge of their own selection process and timing, of what fits when, which in itself is another empowering possibility absent in dysfunctional families.

Exploring this workbook will be an adventure, bound to open new pathways to self and others in ways which enhance self-esteem and healthy relationships. I hope that Jesse and Pat will go on to write many more.

Bunny S. Duhl
Cambridge, MA

June 1990

PREFACE

We designed this book for any couple who wants to build or improve upon a healthy, joyful relationship. The exercises cover a range of issues and encourage each partner to deal with unresolved problems.

If in working through these exercises you or your partner find that you are struggling — that you have reached a "stuck point" and are unable to resolve your problems — you may want to seek help. If so, seek this help from a professional person specializing in the treatment of couples.

However, whether used on your own or with the help of a therapist, it is our hope that the various activities included in this booklet will serve you in building bridges to intimacy. We intend that you recognize and value both separateness and togetherness as necessary ingredients of a healthy relationship. We believe that both you and your partner will:

- improve the quantity and quality of your communication with each other;

- explore each of your family backgrounds;

- identify ways your family histories are affecting your current functioning;

- examine overlooked boundary issues;

- recognize and build upon the strengths in your relationship;

- view your differences as resources; and

- introduce (or re-introduce) playfulness and spontaneity into your life as a couple.

In whatever order or setting you use these exercises we want you to discover new facets of your relationship. We know that you will find joy from working through your problems together.

Part A
PARTNERS: AN INTRODUCTION

Partners in successful intimate relationships share many experiences. This is also true for those partnerships which break apart. We have noted that certain of these shared experiences occur in clusters and sequence, (i.e., stages). These stages must be successfully negotiated by couples if they are to unite in a healthy, pleasing and intimate way. They are termed *romantic, disenchantment, productive, second separation and re-integration* stages.[*]

It is helpful to know about these stages so that we will look at our partners with perspective and not run away or fault them or ourselves. Togetherness and separateness are both integral parts of intimacy. If we know this, our experiencing of differences and temporary distancing can be times for pleasure. If we don't know this, the important periods of differentiation in ourselves and in our partners will be unsettling and frightening.

THE ROMANTIC STAGE

During the romantic or honeymoon stage couples emphasize togetherness; they tend to "fuse" together as an entity and become a couple. Throughout this period there is often joy at discovering one another.

During this stage, however, it is not uncommon for some to give up boundaries or repress their values in order to maintain the relationship. In a sense they deny who they are or what they feel in order to keep their relationship intact.

Another common occurrence in this stage is for one partner to see the other as more of a "savior" than as an equal. This is illustrated by individuals who believe that their partner has "saved" them from their families, poverty or other especially undesirable situations. However, constructing a relationship on the basis of compensation, denial or being saved is not a sound basis for developing a healthy, joyful and intimate team.

All individuals have unique needs and attributes. If people ignore too many of their individual characteristics they blind themselves. They make it difficult to make a smooth transition into the second stage, the disenchantment stage. Worse, they are likely to arrive at the second stage prematurely (i.e., before they have adequately bonded to one another).

Several of the exercises in this book are intended to facilitate this bonding or fusion of you with another, while maintaining your integrity as a unique human being.

---

[*]For a more in depth review of theory and research concerning these stages see in the *Bibliography* Campbell, 1980; Hendricks and Hendricks, 1987; Kramer, 1985; Scarff, 1987; and Schwartz and Schwartz, 1980.

THE DISENCHANTMENT STAGE

In every successful intimate relationship the participants experience mutual trust, commitment, understanding and respect while they struggle through their concerns. They see differences between themselves for what they are--simply differences. Nonetheless in every healthy intimate relationship a certain amount of disenchantment occurs. This disenchantment can grow to the point of breaking the relationship or it can be reduced. It can even become the basis for increased caring and loving if differences are understood and respected.

Divergent views over child-rearing, finances, together-time/alone-time, color schemes, sexual issues, or whatever, are not necessarily ominous. Usually they can be settled according to what best fits the needs of both instead of the one who has the most power. If partners do not do the necessary groundwork to resolve their disagreements they will stick together out of guilt, convenience, economic necessity or emotional dependency. If that is the case, however, there will be an overdose of pain and little joy.

To complicate matters, if people learn as children to cope with disagreements in a dysfunctional way, that mode of coping is likely to be repeated. If they do not change their habits they are likely to replicate many of the problems they experienced in their families of origin.

It is difficult for some to see conflict and differences of opinion as normal. This is usually not due to a lack of love, but to a search for self. Unfortunately, however, disagreement is often mistaken as a turning away, and divorce is not uncommon at this stage.

Those who hang together with a kind of "white knuckle" dependence on dysfunctional problem solving skills are weakening the fabric of their relationship. This, in turn, retards their movement through the next stages. Unless partners can welcome, or at least allow for differences, trust and cohesion are impossible. During this time, enlisting the aid of a professional who is knowledgeable about recovery and family of origin issues might be a wise investment. Individual family of origin work is recommended.

Whether professional help is sought or not, we all need to realize that letting go of illusions and inappropriate expectations is an important part of a healthy and joyful relationship. By letting go, we can *relax* and be proud of being a member of a team. We will also be better prepared for stage three--the productive stage.

THE PRODUCTIVE STAGE

If any serious threat of separation is ended and partners have the ability to appreciate and resolve their differences, they usually will give up seeking power over the other. They then enter a new phase, the productive stage. Here, mutual interests are revived or introduced and each actively supports one another in new ways. Parenting classes, couples' therapy or workshops which teach communication and boundary setting skills may be in order. Such resources can teach couples how to put aside childhood roles and take responsibility for pulling together.

Conflicts will occur but differences of opinion will not be as threatening as in the preceding stage. There will be less likelihood of blaming the other and more willingness to accept responsibility. Partners forgive and are forgiven. Children, careers, home and travel may again stimulate functioning as a team.

Yet here again, those who have grown up in dysfunctional homes may not act as a team. They may not know how to give emotional support. Without healthy role models to imitate, they are likely to lack the awareness and skills for functioning as a healthy couple. If this is true, it is important for them to resolve any personal problems stemming from childhood. Many of the exercises in this book provide for joint efforts at resolving problems that were developed in childhood.

SECOND SEPARATION

Usually a second separation stage occurs when couples are in their forties, yet it can occur at other ages. When a second separation occurs it will be quite unsettling, for it will be a time of serious *psychological* separation. To successfully pass through it requires reclamation, expression, and a recognition of disowned aspects of self which were earlier attributed to the partner.

If the other stages of a relationship have not been mastered, this will be a very fragile time. Trust will be low and the temptation to run, to cling to others, or to control others will be high. At this stage it is especially important that each partner emphasize concern for the other's needs. It is important to create a context where one's deepest and most subtle feelings find expression. If partners do this, they will rejoice in their sense of wholeness. If couples fail to develop mutually acceptable self-definitions, there will be a permanent split or a dependent kind of clinging together. Such clinging together will be stifling and hamper moving into the next and final stage of successful intimacy--the re-integration stage.

RE-INTEGRATION STAGE

This period is marked by renewed appreciation for the other. Each partner has a sense of self-respect, self-trust and recommitment and extends these feelings to the other. Neither partner **needs** the other, yet **chooses** to enhance and be enhanced by the other. Two well-developed people come together and bring excitement to their relationship. They emphasize the "we" aspect of the relationship. Each values the partnership as being good for both.

Often there is a rekindling of romance and an increase in sexual desire and performance. Disagreements will occur, but they will be based on genuine differences. And there will be a "win-win" quality in their efforts to come together on an issue. There is little need to punish, for the need to control the other has subsided.

Yet, working toward a healthy and joyful intimate relationship is never over. There will always be new issues to share. New roles will emerge, such as in-laws, grandparents, consultants, retirees or whatever. There will be new limitations due to aging, changes in financial condition, accidents or other events. And, of course, each of us will have new traumas to face, such as the death of one's parents or children.

Thus, the boundaries of a joyful and intimate relationship are constantly being refined and negotiated. The rhythm and flow of togetherness and separateness will continue, but this can be rewarding. Partners will tap into each other for **courage, compassion, empathy** and **tolerance**. Each sustains the good relationship. Mutual courage, compassion, empathy, and tolerance make up the structure of each couple's bridge to intimacy.

> Each of the following exercises teaches one to enjoy loving and being loved. They enhance capacities for love and life. They are activities for building bridges to a joyful and caring relationship.

Part B
FAMILIES OF ORIGIN*

Virginia Satir (1983) emphasized what wise people have noted: parents are our most powerful teachers. She calls them the "architects of the family," and maintained that on the basis of one's experience in the family one learns how to fit into the world and how much trust to put into relationships with others. For most of us, our parents have passed on much of what we have become. If what they have given us hurts us, then we need to intervene and make changes in ourselves.

Our goal in the next few exercises is to provide a way of understanding the family backgrounds of you and your partner. The more aware you are of the rules and roles you have inherited, the more enlightened choices you will make. You will take a new look at your old ways, and from an emerging and enlightened perspective, consciously change to more healthy and joyful ways of living.

The following exercises are excellent tools for identifying past family values, patterns, and communication styles. The worksheets will provide you with guidelines for detecting important aspects of family life. For example, did your family keep dangerous secrets, avoid conflict, favor males, or put you or your brothers or sisters in surrogate spouse positions? If so, they probably caused you many problems.

It is important, however, to note that not all current problems stem from your past. Furthermore, not all family of origin messages are unhealthy, even those from fundamentally unhealthy families. Nonetheless, a discerning "close-up" view of backgrounds is likely to be useful as you modify or discard what gets in your way of developing a healthy relationship. Couples should decide together what they want to perpetuate in their relationship and what they hope to transmit to others, such as offspring, friends, or other family members.

We will also want to take a look at what may have been missing in your family history and work to achieve what is lacking yet valued. For example, if you find heaviness and a lack of humor in your original families, you may decide to acquire a playful attitude. Whatever you seek, the exercises are intended to propel you toward healing and change.

---

*We recommend Satir, 1983; Satir and Baldwin, 1983; and James Framo in Kramer, 1985, for a discussion of the importance of one's family background. Please see *Bibliography*.

Exercise 1

Roots: Family of Origin Maps

PURPOSE:

This map exercise will provide you with an opportunity to view your own and your partner's family from a new perspective. It is designed to:

- record the unique history of each partner;

- expand insights into family members and to "flesh them out" as persons;

- reveal inter-generational family patterns;

- identify ways family history affects current relationships; and

- set in motion the process of healing and change.

Reviewing the maps together can provide an understanding of each other's behavior and help each of you take a new look at the source of those behaviors. Against the backdrop of such information, a decision to retain or change certain behavior patterns can be made.

TASK:

On a separate sheet of paper, each partner should prepare a family map--a graphic picture of his or her family or origin. Include parents, siblings, miscarriages, abortions, and any people who lived with your family (relative or non-relative). Also include dogs, cats, or other significant pets.

Your name is to be placed in the middle of the circle. **Place a star in your circle.**

Put the names or nicknames of others at the top of each circle. Include each person's birth date and current age or date of death. Indicate marriage date (and divorce or separation date, if applicable) for parents. Then add place of birth, ethnic background, occupations, religious preference, level of formal education, illnesses (medical and psychological, including addictions), and cause of death, if applicable. Draw a diagonal through any deceased members of your family.

Now indicate the degree of closeness, distance or conflict in the various relationships. For a very close relationship, draw three parallel lines (≡), for a distant relationship use a broken line (– – –), and for a conflictual relationship use an up and down line (∧∧∧). Write down five adjectives to describe each family member and non-family member who lived with your family or who spent a lot of time there--including yourself. If there were miscarriages, abortions, or stillborns, describe your fantasy of what they would have been like had they lived. When you finish, your picture may resemble the one in Figure 1.

At the top of the map, write three words which describe the *relationship* of the partners as perceived by you while growing up, or as told to you by others if you did not know them as a couple.

Following the same instructions, make a map of your maternal and paternal grandparents. See Figure 2 and Figure 3.

Figure 1
Family of Origin

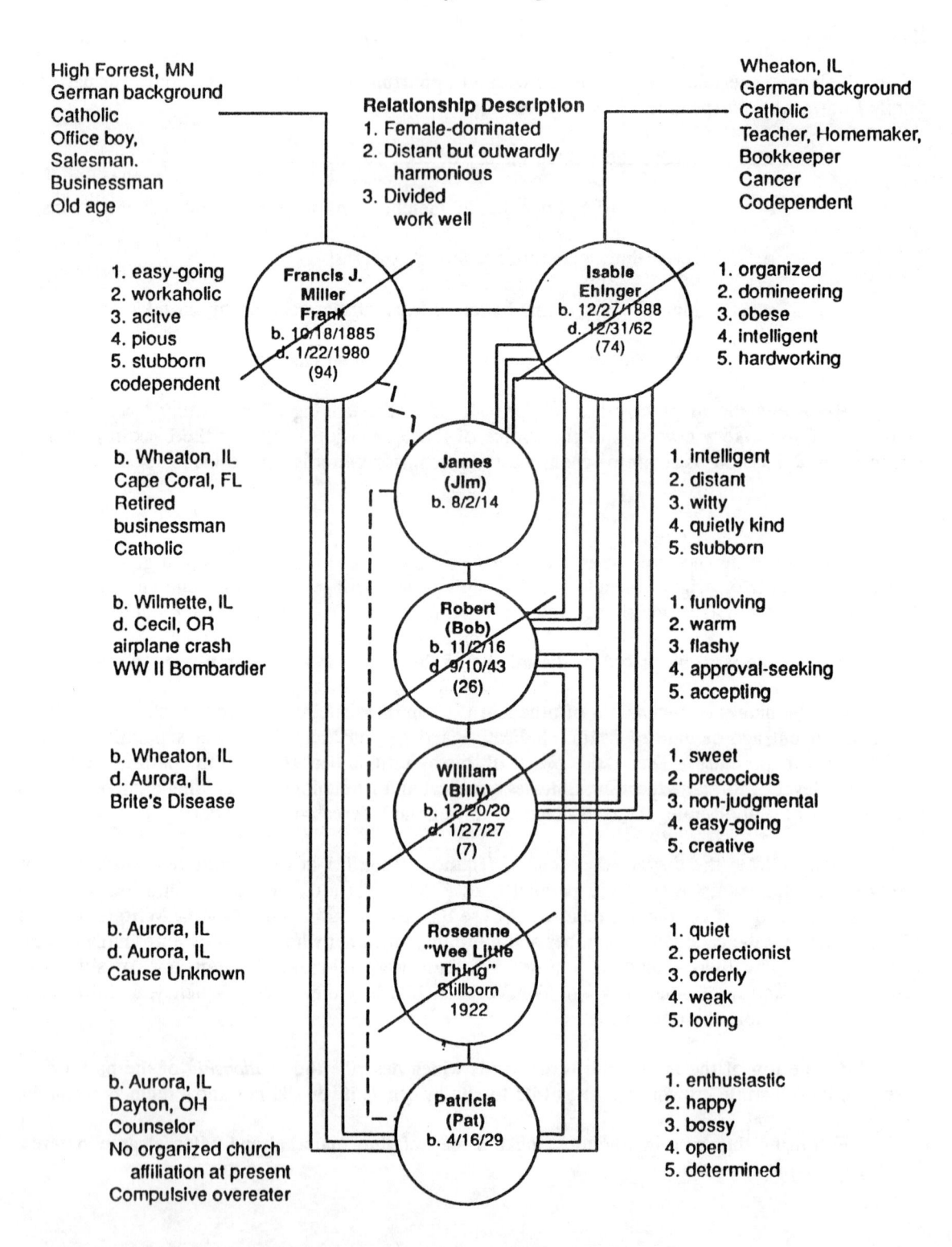

Relationship Description
1. Female-dominated
2. Distant but outwardly harmonious
3. Divided work well

Francis J. Miller "Frank"
b. 10/18/1885
d. 1/22/1980
(94)

High Forrest, MN
German background
Catholic
Office boy,
Salesman,
Businessman
Old age

1. easy-going
2. workaholic
3. acitve
4. pious
5. stubborn
codependent

Isable Ehinger
b. 12/27/1888
d. 12/31/62
(74)

Wheaton, IL
German background
Catholic
Teacher, Homemaker,
Bookkeeper
Cancer
Codependent

1. organized
2. domineering
3. obese
4. intelligent
5. hardworking

James (Jim)
b. 8/2/14

b. Wheaton, IL
Cape Coral, FL
Retired
businessman
Catholic

1. intelligent
2. distant
3. witty
4. quietly kind
5. stubborn

Robert (Bob)
b. 11/2/16
d. 9/10/43
(26)

b. Wilmette, IL
d. Cecil, OR
airplane crash
WW II Bombardier

1. funloving
2. warm
3. flashy
4. approval-seeking
5. accepting

William (Billy)
b. 12/20/20
d. 1/27/27
(7)

b. Wheaton, IL
d. Aurora, IL
Brite's Disease

1. sweet
2. precocious
3. non-judgmental
4. easy-going
5. creative

Roseanne "Wee Little Thing"
Stillborn
1922

b. Aurora, IL
d. Aurora, IL
Cause Unknown

1. quiet
2. perfectionist
3. orderly
4. weak
5. loving

Patricia (Pat)
b. 4/16/29

b. Aurora, IL
Dayton, OH
Counselor
No organized church
  affiliation at present
Compulsive overeater

1. enthusiastic
2. happy
3. bossy
4. open
5. determined

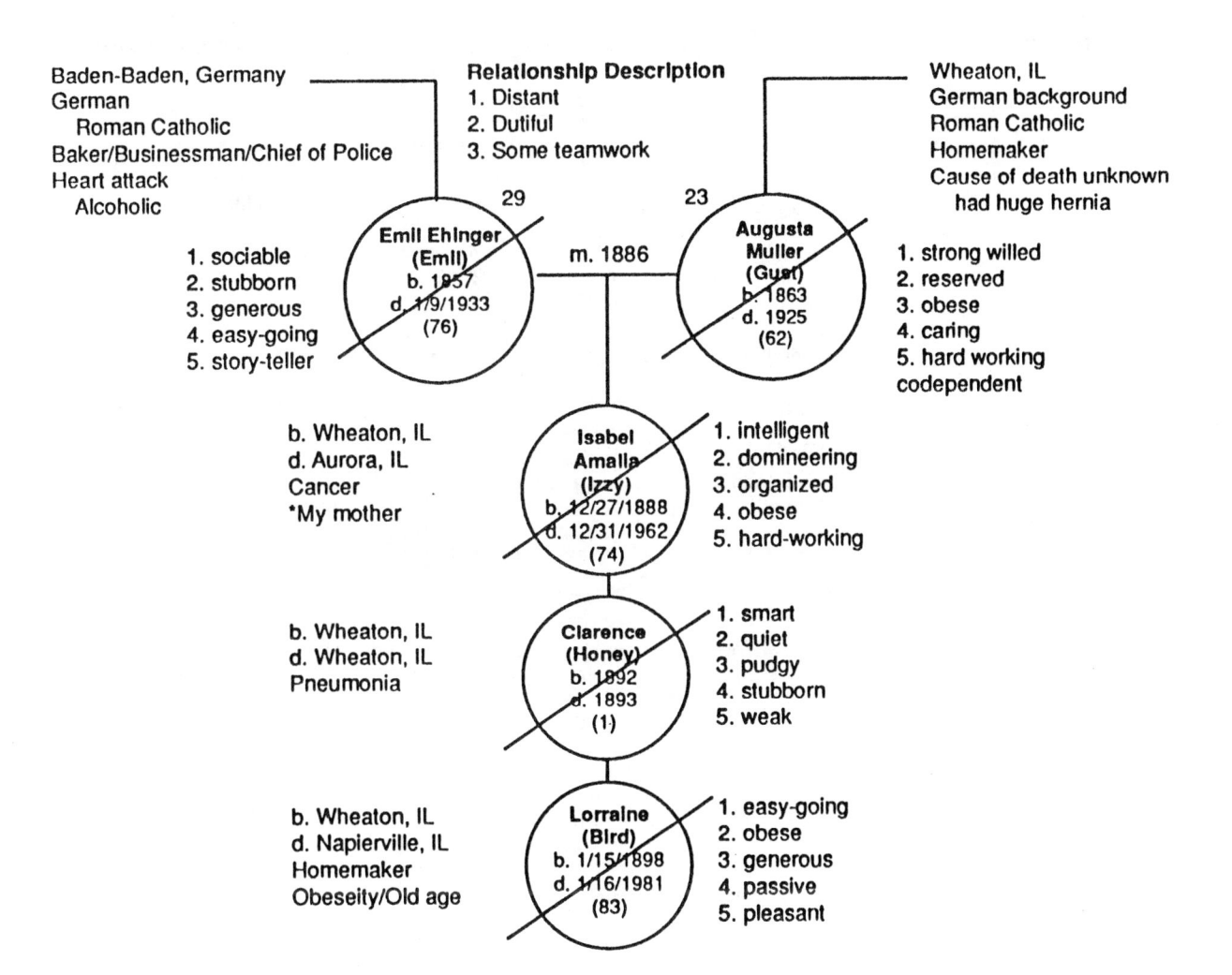

Figure 2
Maternal Grandparents

Relationship Description
1. Distant
2. Dutiful
3. Some teamwork

Baden-Baden, Germany
German
  Roman Catholic
Baker/Businessman/Chief of Police
Heart attack
  Alcoholic

Wheaton, IL
German background
Roman Catholic
Homemaker
Cause of death unknown
  had huge hernia

Emil Ehinger (Emil)
b. 1857
d. 1/9/1933
(76)

m. 1886   29 / 23

Augusta Muller (Gust)
b. 1863
d. 1925
(62)

Emil:
1. sociable
2. stubborn
3. generous
4. easy-going
5. story-teller

Augusta:
1. strong willed
2. reserved
3. obese
4. caring
5. hard working
codependent

b. Wheaton, IL
d. Aurora, IL
Cancer
*My mother

Isabel Amalia (Izzy)
b. 12/27/1888
d. 12/31/1962
(74)

1. intelligent
2. domineering
3. organized
4. obese
5. hard-working

b. Wheaton, IL
d. Wheaton, IL
Pneumonia

Clarence (Honey)
b. 1892
d. 1893
(1)

1. smart
2. quiet
3. pudgy
4. stubborn
5. weak

b. Wheaton, IL
d. Napierville, IL
Homemaker
Obesity/Old age

Lorraine (Bird)
b. 1/15/1898
d. 1/16/1981
(83)

1. easy-going
2. obese
3. generous
4. passive
5. pleasant

Figure 3
Paternal Grandparents

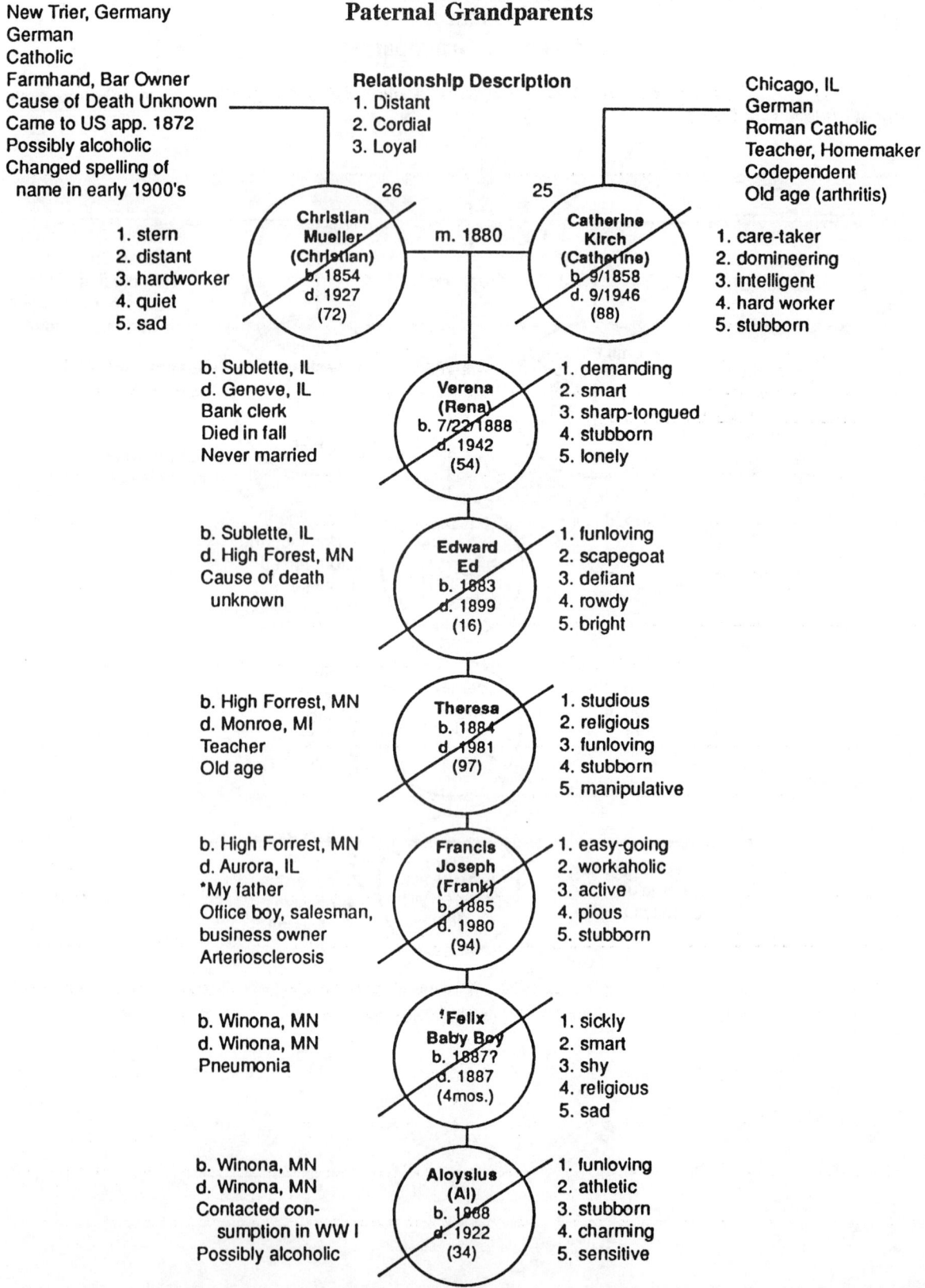

Relationship Description
1. Distant
2. Cordial
3. Loyal

New Trier, Germany
German
Catholic
Farmhand, Bar Owner
Cause of Death Unknown
Came to US app. 1872
Possibly alcoholic
Changed spelling of
  name in early 1900's

Chicago, IL
German
Roman Catholic
Teacher, Homemaker
Codependent
Old age (arthritis)

Christian Mueller (Christian)
b. 1854
d. 1927
(72)
— 26 — m. 1880 — 25 —
Catherine Kirch (Catherine)
b. 9/1858
d. 9/1946
(88)

Christian:
1. stern
2. distant
3. hardworker
4. quiet
5. sad

Catherine:
1. care-taker
2. domineering
3. intelligent
4. hard worker
5. stubborn

Verena (Rena)
b. 7/22/1888
d. 1942
(54)

b. Sublette, IL
d. Geneve, IL
Bank clerk
Died in fall
Never married

1. demanding
2. smart
3. sharp-tongued
4. stubborn
5. lonely

Edward Ed
b. 1883
d. 1899
(16)

b. Sublette, IL
d. High Forest, MN
Cause of death unknown

1. funloving
2. scapegoat
3. defiant
4. rowdy
5. bright

Theresa
b. 1884
d. 1981
(97)

b. High Forrest, MN
d. Monroe, MI
Teacher
Old age

1. studious
2. religious
3. funloving
4. stubborn
5. manipulative

Francis Joseph (Frank)
b. 1885
d. 1980
(94)

b. High Forrest, MN
d. Aurora, IL
*My father
Office boy, salesman, business owner
Arteriosclerosis

1. easy-going
2. workaholic
3. active
4. pious
5. stubborn

---

†Felix Baby Boy
b. 1887?
d. 1887
(4mos.)

b. Winona, MN
d. Winona, MN
Pneumonia

1. sickly
2. smart
3. shy
4. religious
5. sad

Aloysius (Al)
b. 1888
d. 1922
(34)

b. Winona, MN
d. Winona, MN
Contacted consumption in WW I
Possibly alcoholic

1. funloving
2. athletic
3. stubborn
4. charming
5. sensitive

Compare your map with your partner's. What stands out?

1. Compare the size of your families. If there are big differences in family size, what impact might this have?

_____

_____

_____

_____

2. Look at your sibling position and your partner's sibling position. What impact might birth order have on how you relate to each other? (For example, two oldest children are likely to encounter issues with power and control.)

_____

_____

_____

_____

3. What role did you play in your family and how does this role fit with your partner's role?

_____

_____

_____

_____

4. Look at the number of male and female children as well as the gender birth order in your respective families. What effect might that have on how you relate to your partner?

_____

_____

_____

_____

5. What characteristics first attracted you to your mate? Does anyone in your family or origin display these characteristics? If so, who?

_____
_____
_____
_____

6. Look at the degree of closeness, distance, and conflict in your family of origin. What impact might this have in your current relationship with your spouse? (Pay particular attention to the relationship between your mother and father.)

_____
_____
_____
_____

7. What did you learn in your family or origin about how to get power, how to be close and how to feel about yourself?

_____
_____
_____
_____

8. Who in your family told others what to do?

_____
_____
_____
_____

9. How did you go about getting what you wanted and are these coping methods the same now as they were then?

_____
_____
_____
_____
_____

10. What was going on, historically, in your city, in the nation, in the world, at the time of your birth? Did this have an effect on your growing-up years? On how you act now?

_____
_____
_____
_____
_____

11. Did religious, ethnic, and socioeconomic similarities or differences add strengths or stresses to your parents' lives and to yours?

_____
_____
_____
_____

12. Which family relationship from the past, if any, does your current partnership most resemble?

_____
_____
_____
_____
_____

Exercise 2
Photographs: "Hey, Look Me Over..."*

PURPOSE:

Family photographs are important documents. By using family photographs, you will:

- **Evoke** memories of past events and relationships.

- **Uncover** feelings about these events and relationships.

- **Identify** periods of family stress (often indicated by fewer pictures).

- **Discover** divergences from the usual (e.g., firstborns are photographed more).

- **Provide** factual, historical information.

- **Reveal** the power or importance of certain family members (e.g., more pictures, larger size photos, special medium (oils), etc.)

- **Illuminate** different values, interests and talents of the photographer and those photographed.

- **Affirm** a sense of identity and separateness.

TASKS:

1. Each partner gathers photographs (or movies) of themselves and their family members which say something important about the relationships among the family members. If possible, include 25-30 pictures which cover three generations.

As you look at the pictures, notice the following:

- physical closeness and distance among family members;

- degree of seriousness or playfulness portrayed;

- present or absent members (1, 2, or 3 generations present?);

- conflictual/harmonious relationships, repetitive behavior, family structure (Who stands near whom? Who "acts up" at picture-taking time? Who is the "black sheep"? Does someone consistently hide behind others or sit down to hide weight gains/losses?);

- themes evident or recurrent: power, dependency, tensions, intimacy, equality, and perfectionism.

---

*Adapted from Anderson, Carol and Malloy, Elaine. "Family photographs: in treatment and training," *Family Process*, (1976), 15, 259-264.

2. Now share the results of your treasure hunt. Discuss with your partner:

- reasons why you selected these particular photos;
- meaning the pictures have (particular subjects, gestures, stances);
- emotional reactions to the pictures (e.g., sad, happy, angry, scared);
- which family member dominated (e.g., more photos or presented first or last).
- condition of the photos or movies (Have they been cared for?);
- whole family photographs (Are there any?)
- speed of sharing photos with your partner.

3. List three new learnings or awarenesses:

_____
_____
_____
_____
_____
_____

Exercise 3

Looking Back

PURPOSE:

    Keeping secrets, and the inability to express feelings, are common characteristics of troubled couples. Yet many couples fail to recognize that childhood experiences are important to how they cope with issues in their relationship today.

    This exercise provides a structure for couples to break unhealthy patterns and to risk sharing vulnerability--a necessary component of trust and intimacy.

TASK:

    1.   Describe below how you and your partner met. Include any circumstances which you feel are important:

_____

_____

_____

_____

_____

    2.   What was the length of your "courtship?"

_____

_____

_____

_____

_____

    3.   What are the main characteristics that attracted you to your mate?

_____

_____

_____

_____

4. Are any of these characteristics now a source of difficulty between the two of you?

___

5. In what ways do the two of you complement or balance each other?

___

6. If the decision to marry was made, what was the response of each of you?

___

7. Why did you decide to make the commitment and do you feel that each made this commitment for the same reasons?

___

8. Are there discrepancies in what you and your mate remember about the decision to join together?

_____
_____
_____
_____
_____

9. Was the commitment to each other made during a time of severe emotional stress, or was it made in a calm and rational manner?

_____
_____
_____
_____
_____

10. Were there any significant events prior to your committment to each other (e.g., divorce or death of parent) which might have affected your decision to marry?

_____
_____
_____
_____
_____

Reflections on this Exercise

Write down the feelings which surfaced as you discussed the above questions. Record any insights, changes or similarities in how you operate as a pair today.

_____
_____
_____

Exercise 4

Relationship Path

PURPOSE:

This activity will reveal your shared history as a couple and will provide an opportunity for you to work together as a team. In addition, you will discover the meaning each partner places on past events, and the strengths you have to help you through the tough times.

TASK:

On a large sheet of paper, draw the path of your relationship. The outline may look similar to the sample on the next page. Use PICTURES as well as WORDS to fill in the following data:

1. **The Meeting:** Describe your beginning as a couple,

   - **When** did you meet?
   - **Where** did you meet?
   - **How** did you meet?
   - **Who** was there?
   - **What** stood out about that first meeting?

2. **Define Turning Points:** Identify 4-5 major turning points in your relationship. Indicate whether these involve one or both of you, and how these changes affected the relationship.

   - Label and date each turning point.
   - Draw a picture to represent the turning points.
   - Look at each turning point. Did you create it, (e.g., quit a job) or was it externally initiated and out of your control (e.g., death of a child)? Note this in some way on your map.

3. **Major Periods:**

   - Label and date four or five major periods in your relationship (e.g., getting acquainted, turbulent period, growing gulf, re-connecting).
   - Select a metaphor (picture or phrase) to characterize each of these major periods.
   - Identify a feeling associated with each phase.

**Figure 4
Our Relationship Path**

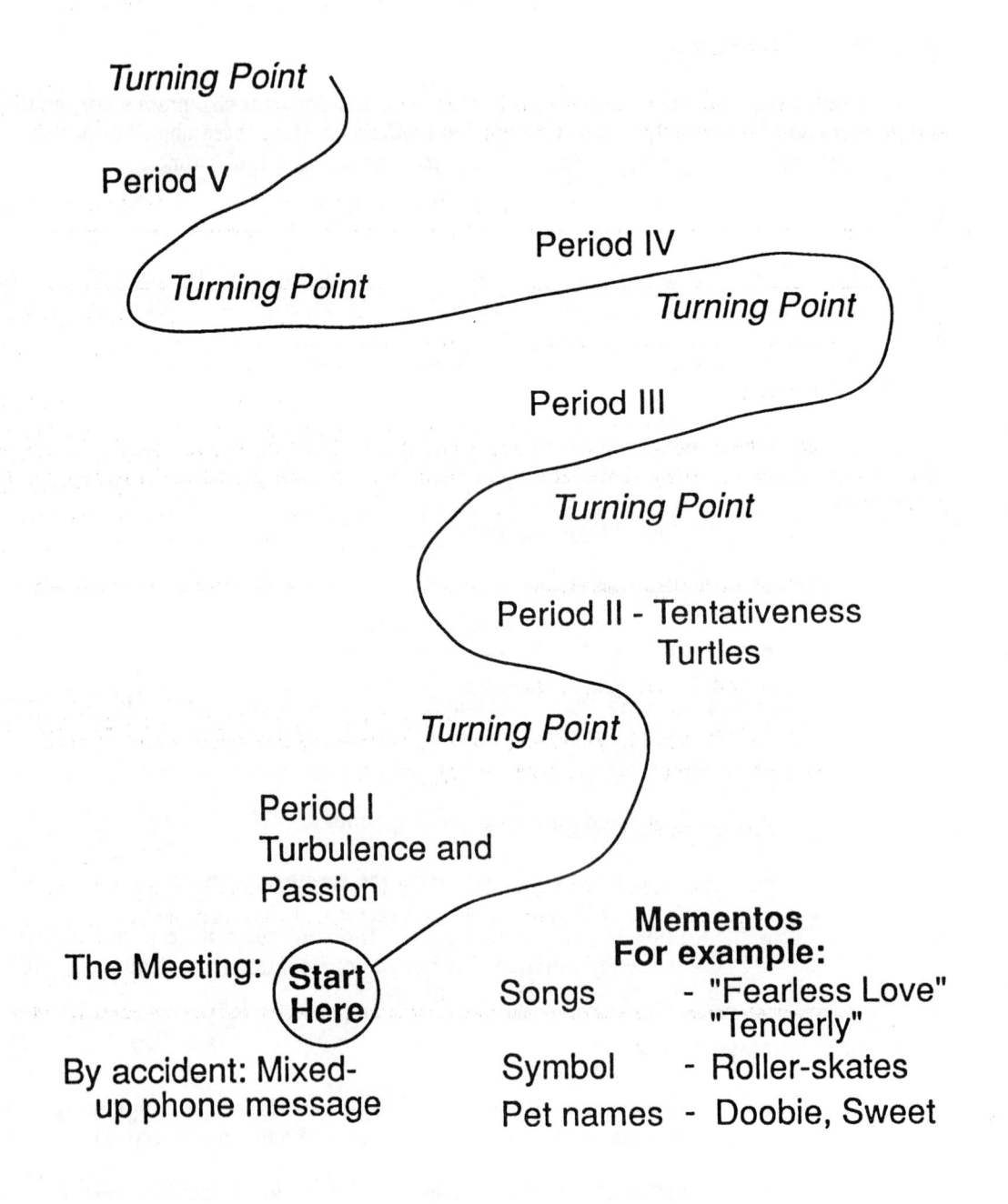

Turning Point

Period V

Turning Point

Period IV

Turning Point

Period III

Turning Point

Period II - Tentativeness
Turtles

Turning Point

Period I
Turbulence and
Passion

The Meeting: **Start Here**

By accident: Mixed-
up phone message

**Mementos
For example:**

Songs   - "Fearless Love"
                 "Tenderly"
Symbol   - Roller-skates
Pet names - Doobie, Sweet

4. **Symbols**

If you have time, place "special mementos" somewhere on the sheet: songs, symbols and phrases which are meaningful to you as a couple.

5. **Strengths:**

Look over your map. Discuss with your mate the particular qualities or strengths (in you and your partner) which helped you through the hard times. List them here.

1. _____   2. _____

3. _____   4. _____

5. _____

6. **Learning**

Each take a separate piece of paper and draw a box (see Wisdom Box). In this box write at least one sentence stating the wisdom you gleaned **from each period and turning point** in your relationship.

WISDOM BOX

Period I: Getting Acquainted:

Getting to know you was like discovering a precious jewel. I need to keep remembering the facets of you which I admire.

Period III: Raising the Kids:

Kids need to be praised. They also need limits. Saying "no" can be loving. Being an effective parent is difficult and time-consuming.

Exercise 5

Relationship Metaphors

PURPOSE:

This exercise is intended to:

- Heighten awareness of how partners see each other.

- Increase objectivity and reduce anxiety by using metaphors to represent the couple.

- Emphasize that personal qualities can have both positive and negative aspects which affect the relationship.

- Uncover recurrent problems, (e.g., control; fear of abandonment) patterns of behavior, and desired changes.

TASK:

Relationship Metaphor #1

- Think of an animal which represents your partner (e.g, owl).

- Think of an animal to represent you (e.g., rabbit).

- Put the animal in a setting (e.g., forest).

- Create a story with a beginning, middle and end. If the animals become involved in repetitive action (e.g., like running after each other in a circle) stop this and allow for some kind of resolution.

Sample: The lively rabbit runs through the forest. It hears the owl hooting. It looks around and sees the soft feathers and penetrating eyes of the owl who is sitting on the limb of a tree. The rabbit winks and waves, then scampers off. The owl hoots again. The rabbit is scared--but hops closer to the tree and looks up again. The owl doesn't seem as formidable as first perceived. The rabbit quiets down, climbs the tree, slowly approaches and sits beside the owl. They begin to talk and share with one another.

Processing Guidelines

1. Pull out the major elements in your story (e.g., owl, rabbit, forest, tree).

2. Write three or more adjectives for each of the major elements.

Example:

> owl — soft, penetrating, formidable (warmer when rabbit close)
> perched high — rabbit comes to her level

> rabbit — lively, responsive, scared, risk-taking
> tree — tall, stately, strong

3. Share the story and adjectives with your partner. (Your partner may ask you to fill in details).

4. Discuss the following with your partner:

   - What familiar issues or patterns stand out in the story? (For instance, the rabbit in the above story admits to not slowing down enough at times to see and accept love when it is offered).

   - What behavior does each animal display which contributes to the patterns in the story? (The owl often hoots when he really wants to reach out!)

   - What do you think each animal is wanting?

   - How could each of the adjectives be a strength **and** a liability?

   - Did the animals' interaction in any way resemble your parents' or grandparents' relationship?

   - What strengths are apparent in your story?

   - What changes could **each** animal make to alter any problematic pattern?

Relationship Metaphor #2
(a variation of the animal metaphor)

Write a metaphor to describe your relationship as you see it now.

For example:

> "I see my mate as a sweater which continually unravels and needs repair. I am the frustrated repair person who keeps noticing the imperfections and tries to keep fixing it, even though I don't feel I'm very good at sewing. The sweater is still functional but it's not perfect."

Use the Processing Guidelines 1 and 2 as with metaphor #1.

Share the description with your partner and discuss the following questions:

- How could each of the adjectives be a strength and a deficit?

- Does the metaphor describe the relationship when it is smooth or when it is stressful?

- What did you like about the description?

- What change(s) in the description of your self would you like to make?

Exercise 6

Memories

PURPOSE:

Many of the problems we experience in current relationships stem from experiences in our family of origin. If we can identify and work through these earlier feelings and perceptions, we are often better able to work through current relationship struggles as well. That is the goal of this exercise.

TASK:

1. Identify a current problem or struggle you are having in your relationship. Explain:

   _____
   _____
   _____
   _____
   _____

2. If you were to approach your partner with this problem, what would your partner say or do?

   _____
   _____
   _____
   _____

3. When was the first time you ever experienced a struggle of this kind? With whom? Where were you? What was happening? Record your earliest memory.

   _____
   _____
   _____
   _____
   _____

4. Discuss each of the above responses with your partner. What are the areas in which the two of you agree and disagree?

_____

_____

_____

_____

_____

Exercise 7

The Interpersonal Vulnerability Contract[*]

PURPOSE:

All people have experienced incidents in childhood when they felt helpless, scared, or unsafe. Adults carry more than their share of such experiences. As a result of these troublesome incidents, we develop defenses to try to protect ourselves. Yet these protections, paradoxically, often produce negative experiences. This activity helps partners to identify their own vulnerabilities and protections. It also encourages them to develop and contract to carry out alternative methods to deal with stressful events.

TASK:

This is a powerful activity and can have an enormously positive impact on the relationship. Complete each of the following sections. Use the examples to help you in your responses.

1. **Identifying vulnerabilities:**

   What were the toughest things you had to cope with in your family of origin?

   _____

   _____

   _____

   _____

   For example:

   I was never heard.

   I wasn't allowed to ask questions.

   I was told by others how I felt.

   I was supposed to be perfect, and didn't know how.

   I was isolated, excluded and didn't belong.

   I was always criticized, judged, and not accepted.

   I felt I had to be in control because no one else was.

   I never knew what was happening; no one would tell me.

---

[*]Revised and condensed by permission of the author Bunny S. Duhl, Ed. D. Boston Family Institute, Brookline, MA, 1976. *The Interpersonal Vulnerability Contract* was presented at the First Family Encounter, November 1976, Mexico City, Mexico.

Note: Vulnerabilities usually involve some element of loss. Are you still sensitive to those same types of situations? Which ones?

_____

_____

_____

_____

2. **Couples' Exercise:**

- Choose one of the toughest things you had to cope with (from section above) and share it with your partner.

- Decide which partner will be the storyteller and which will be the listener.

- The listener asks the storyteller to discuss "the tough situation" in detail. Be empathic and gentle as your partner re-experiences the pain.

- Validate the pain of those experiences. Do not try to fix or solve the problem. Simply listen.

- Acknowledge what you hear, see and feel as you listen:

    I see ...

    I hear ...

    I feel (in response) ...

    a. emotion

    b. sensation

- The listening partner relates how much of this story, this pain, she or he had known, and how much is new information.

- Ask: "What didn't you know then that you needed to know in order not to be scared? What did you need to see, to hear, to ask, or to tell in order to feel more certain; and to master the situation?"

3. **Present Vulnerabilities:**

   What do you currently consider to be upsetting or vulnerable situations (e.g., areas where you fear loss of connection, abandonment, isolation, helplessness or pressure to perform)?

   _____

   _____

   _____

   _____

4. **Recognizing Internal Signals**

   Make a list of sensations or symptoms you experience when you feel vulnerable or unsafe.

   Examples:

   My stomach tightens, my palms get sweaty, my throat gets dry.

   My heart beats faster, my muscles get tight, my mind goes blank.

   My mind speeds up in a frenzy, my muscles start twitching, my heart starts pounding.

   _____

   _____

   _____

   _____

   These signals can alert you to the connection between past "devastating" situations and the present event. Awareness of these internal signals can interrupt the defensive behavior associated with vulnerability.

5. **Recognizing External Signals:**

   List your behaviors that **others** see when you are feeling vulnerable or unsafe?

   Examples:

   I get angry, lose perspective, rant and rave.
   I avoid eye contact.
   I get very busy and avoid that person or situation.
   I counterattack and blame the other person.
   I argue and set out to prove how right I am.
   I throw things or hit.
   I walk out.
   I stare.
   I get very quiet and withdrawn.

I get scattered and seem to go around in circles.
I cry and take everything as negative.
I start tapping my foot and hold my shoulders back.
I glare at people and start picking my fingernails.
I frown and stare at the door.

_____

_____

_____

_____

Ask your partner to validate or add to your list.

6. **Process with your partner:**

    - Have these protective maneuvers enabled you to "get over" your vulnerabilities? Explain:

    _____

    _____

    - Would you like to explore some new ways of dealing with those scary, upsetting moments? Explain:

    _____

    _____

    - When you feel vulnerable, what can you do for yourself and what do you need from the other person at that moment? Explain:

    _____

    _____

Example:

If you see any of my signals, **ask** me if I am feeling scared, and I will tell you.

Example:

Do not ask me if I am feeling scared or vulnerable, because I will automatically deny it. Instead, tell me what signals you see or hear. Then I will tell you what is bothering me."

_____

_____

Groundrules for Contracts

Whatever is contracted for must be observable and "do-able" in behavior. "I will try" is not acceptable, for it permits the status quo to remain. Rather, we ask people to state what they really feel they can do, no matter how small a step it is in new behavior.

7. **Contract**

    - For a contract to be successful, each party must take responsibility for new behavior. Carefully explore what you would like to have happen at your most vulnerable moments. The new behaviors of **both** parties should be part of this contract.

Example:

"I will acknowledge that I feel vulnerable. However, I will need to wait until later to tell you what it's about, because I just can't talk at that moment."

Note: For some, the "later" should be contracted to take place within the next 24 hours. For others, that kind of time delay is intolerable and the contract may call for a few minutes to deal with the issue. Other people have reported that as part of their needs to be spelled out in a contract, they wished to be physically left alone for a while before dealing with the issue. Others may indicate a need to be held, with or without discussion, right then.

- Specify what you then would like your partner to do?

Example:

"I would like my partner to ask me if I'm feeling overwhelmed and to give me a hug. I will take a deep breath and some time out to get in touch with myself and then come back to my partner and report what I'm feeling and thinking."

_____

_____

_____

- If your partner sees that you are feeling unsafe or vulnerable, what would you like him or her to do or say to check if this perception is correct? And then what will you do?

_____

_____

_____

_____

_____

Part C
OUR CONTACTS WITH EACH OTHER

Contact means "being in touch with" and is based on both sensory awareness and behavior towards someone or something. When we make contact we are able to maintain awareness of the boundary that differentiates "me" from the "other." We must use all of our senses as we make contact with our partners. But by this, we do not mean the simple dictionary definition of contact. In a sense, it is more like the use of the word contact in electricity. Here, the emphasis is on energy exchange. Our feelings and our beliefs which constitute a major source of our feelings are extremely important to share with our partners. Certain habitual patterns may interfere with good contact such as projection, retroflection, and confluence.

In "projection" we avoid owning and knowing parts of ourselves. It is characterized by lots of "you shoulds," blaming and moralizing. When projecting we often fill in the gaps when we are with someone who does not share our feelings or thoughts.

"Retroflection," on the other hand, is evidenced by energy containment. Here we do not share feelings or thoughts. Those who retroflect tend to keep their concerns to themselves, excessively value privacy and tend to withdraw from others.

In "confluence" we act as if we think, and feel exactly the same as the other when we do not. Lots of pleasing and placating takes place and differences are avoided. Those who act this way overvalue agreement and avoid conflict.

Many persons raised in dysfunctional settings are affected by the survival rules learned in childhood (e.g., "don't touch" and "don't talk" rules). When this happens retroflection or confluence occur. "Don't feel" rules tend to restrict expressions of anger, fear, joy, affection, sadness. This can result in projection, retroflection and confluence.

In order to increase our contact, not only with others but ourselves as well, Zinker and Nevis (1981) recommend that we practice:

1. verbalizing our awareness of internal sensations (e.g., "stomach clenched"),

2. voicing our awareness of feelings or thoughts (e.g., "I had a terrible day today."),

3. stating what we notice in our partners (e.g., "Your eyes are droopy. You look tired."),

4. allowing ourselves to voice curiosity about our partner's world (e.g., "How was your meeting today?"),

5. being aware when we say things like "I guess" or "I'll try" or "That's sort of what I mean". Such statements are likely signs of confluence. At such times, it is suggested that we practice airing our disagreements,

6. being alert that our failure to carry out agreements and plans may be a sign that our goal was not mutually owned and that our contact was poor. We need to be concerned whether we agreed to avoid conflict, and

7. reviewing how you work together, summarize what you did well and what you need to improve upon.

In order to practice the above, we must take the risk of breaking some old habits. This may create anxiety which we will have to manage. One way to manage this anxiety is to address our fears as they rise.

Some couples will need to reach out for professional assistance if they become highly emotional during this practice or if breakdowns in communication occur. Other couples will be able to work through problems on their own.

In an attempt to reduce any blockage several exercises follow which are aimed at improving contact.

Exercise 8

Interpersonal Contact Survey*

PURPOSE:

Certain elements comprise what we call interpersonal contact. By completing this survey, couples can rate their ability to make contact and then discuss differences in their assessment.

TASK I:

Read the following items and respond in terms of how often these statements are true for you. Please be sure to rate all items.

    5 = All the time
    4 = Most of the time
    3 = More often than not
    2 = Occasionally
    1 = Rarely
    0 = Never

(Each partner circles with different color or one circles and the other places a square around the number.)

1.	My spouse and I stay focused on a topic we need to resolve.	5	4	3	2	1	0
2.	When I am angry with my spouse, I express it.	5	4	3	2	1	0
3.	I know what I like and what I don't like.	5	4	3	2	1	0
4.	When we go out, it doesn't matter to me how my spouse looks.	5	4	3	2	1	0
5.	I give up my way of doing something if my spouse strongly objects.	5	4	3	2	1	0
6.	There is nothing to be settled or worked on in my marriage.	5	4	3	2	1	0
7.	My spouse and I communicate in ways in addition to talking.	5	4	3	2	1	0
8.	I have a well-defined set of values and beliefs.	5	4	3	2	1	0
9.	My spouse and I move through our weeks with a fixed and standard schedule.	5	4	3	2	1	0

---

*Reprinted by permission of the author Dr. Jon E. Frew from Frew, Jon E., 1983. "Clarity of boundary conditions in interpersonal contact." *The Gestalt Journal*, Vol. 6, No. 2, p. 117-123.

10.	I am open to new ideas or activities suggested by my spouse.	5	4	3	2	1	0
11.	I feel that I have an individual identity even though I am married.	5	4	3	2	1	0
12.	My spouse and I express our affection through kissing, holding, and caressing	5	4	3	2	1	0
13.*	When I have something important to say to my spouse, I find that I "beat around the bush."	5	4	3	2	1	0
14.*	I find that my spouse and I do not share many areas of interest in common.	5	4	3	2	1	0
15.	On the most important topics, I know where I stand and where my spouse stands.	5	4	3	2	1	0
16.	In many respects, my spouse and I are two very different people.	5	4	3	2	1	0
17.*	In our marriage, things get done my way or they don't get done at all.	5	4	3	2	1	0
18.	When a conflict comes up in our marriage, my spouse and I deal with each other.	5	4	3	2	1	0
19.	I open up my deepest feelings and thoughts to my spouse.	5	4	3	2	1	0
20.	I believe there is a right way and a wrong way to do most things.	5	4	3	2	1	0

Key: Concepts   Item numbers

I-boundary   3, 4, 8, 11, 15, 16, 20
Permeability   5, 10, 17, 19
Common figure   1, 6, 9, 14
Interaction   2, 7, 12, 13, 18

I-boundary: The I-boundary is one's subjective experience of what makes one different from others. This measures how able partners are to respect their own and their partner's individuality.

Permeability: In a healthy person, the I-boundary is not fixed and rigid but is permeable allowing the individual to choose to temporarily relax the I-boundary and allow exchange with others. This gives an indication of how able partners are to allow themselves to be influenced by each other.

---

*Negative wording--reverse scale for scoring.

Interaction: Interpersonal contact occurs through interaction between people. People interact through the senses of touch, smell, sight, audition, taste, speech, and movement. This assesses how able partners are to express affectionate as well as conflictual feelings.

Common figure: Interpersonal contact occurs between people at a point which draws their common interest or experience. This common interest is called a common figure. This attempts to assess how able partners are to choose common topics to discuss, engage in common interests and share time together.

Discussion

1. Compare your scores. Where are your strengths and what do you need to work on?

   _____
   _____
   _____
   _____

2. How are you different in terms of your likes and dislikes, values and beliefs?

   _____
   _____
   _____
   _____

3. Are these differences respected in your relationship?

   _____
   _____
   _____
   _____

4. Do you negotiate your differences well?

   _____
   _____
   _____
   _____

5. Are you open to being influenced and to trying new things?

6. Is there give and take and do you share your deepest feelings?

7. Can you stay on a topic until it is resolved?

8. What is the common ground between you? What mutual values, interests, etc. do you share?

9. Can you freely express anger, affection, fear, or sadness?

_____
_____
_____
_____
_____

10. Is touch permitted and freely given?

_____
_____
_____
_____

TASK II:

Read the following paragraph and then rate how often this paragraph describes what is true in your relationship with your spouse.*

"There are times in my relationship with my spouse that I am more aware of being part of an "us," than I am being a "me." We can allow ourselves to be influenced by one another without concern that we will lose our separate identities. I am willing, at these times, to take my spouse for who she/he is, and I give up any desire to change him/her. Sometimes there is a sense of union at these moments and sometimes there is a sharp appreciation of our differences. This togetherness occurs sometimes when we are loving, sometimes when we are in conflict and other times at points in between. What is common at these moments is that we care about the same thing at the same time. I do have a sense of being separate and I also know that I am part of something more than just me. I feel understood, at these times, with no strong need to say or do anything. While sometimes even a little scary, the feelings I have at these moments are generally those of excitement, liveliness, and contentment."

Write and discuss your reactions below:

_____
_____
_____
_____
_____

Exercise 9

Seeing

PURPOSE:

This exercise challenges partners to learn the skill of simply stating what they observe without prejudice or judgment. This skill can help increase partners' awareness of themselves and their feelings, without being interpretive and inflaming.

TASK:

Sit facing your partner. Study your partner's face. Notice all of the details: hair, shape of the lips, skin color, texture, shape of the eyes, shape of the face, and the expression. Really take your partner in. Pay attention to your breathing as you do this. Close your eyes now and see if you can form an image of your partner's face. Can you picture all the details of your partner's face? Are there gaps in your memory? Open your eyes once again and notice what you missed.

Now take turns stating your observations of each other. **Do not** include evaluations such as "I'm noticing your beautiful smile." Report only visual data such as "I'm noticing that your lips are a pale rosy color." Try to paint your partner's face with descriptive, non-evaluative words.

Discuss the experience when you are through and record your responses to the following questions:

1. How able were you to avoid evaluations and labels (such as "You look worried") and stay with data (e.g., "Your forehead is wrinkled and I notice your eyes are squinted")?

_____
_____
_____
_____
_____

2. Were you able to notice new aspects of your partner's face that perhaps you had overlooked before?

_____
_____
_____
_____
_____

3. How did you feel when your partner focused on you?

_____
_____
_____
_____
_____

4. How did you feel focusing on your partner?

_____
_____
_____
_____
_____

5. How do you think staying with the data and avoiding evaluation and interpretation might strengthen your communication?

_____
_____
_____
_____
_____

Exercise 10

Attending to the Inner Voice

PURPOSE:

If partners are more aware of the deeper message beyond their partner's words, potential problems can be circumvented. This requires skill in listening as opposed to the tendency to react defensively or to hear only superficial messages. It also demands that the person learns to listen to his or her own inner responses. These are skills which do not come easily, especially to those who engage in reactive exchanges with their partners. The following activity offers couples the opportunity to practice the skill of responding to the deeper message.

TASK:

Ask your partner to talk about something of concern to him or her. Your task is to listen beneath the word content to the tone of voice, volume and pitch.

You should look at your partner's posture, breathing and facial expression. Notice the sensations, feelings, or images you experience as you listen. Close your eyes and as you continue to listen, form an image of him or her; that is, form a physical representation or metaphor of the underlying feeling or attitude which comes across to you. Try not to censor any images which come to you.

Example:

"I had an image of you with your head pulled in and your arm shielding your face."

1. What were your spontaneous reactions or fantasies while listening to your partner?

_____

_____

_____

_____

_____

2. How do your inner images compare to what your partner was feeling while speaking?

_____

_____

_____

_____

_____

Exercise 11

Touching

PURPOSE:

For many troubled couples, affectionately touching one another is absent in their relationship. To touch is a potent medium of communication. Rather than miss out on this avenue of expression, partners need to learn how to appropriately and sensitively nurture each other through touching.

The following is a non-threatening activity which helps sensitize partners to each other's touch preferences. It teaches partners to ask for the kinds of touch they want, and heightens their awareness of giving and receiving touch.

TASK:

Partners sit face to face, knees touching. Close your eyes and be aware of your breathing. Breathe in to the count of four, hold to the count of four, then exhale to the count of eight. Allow yourself to be more and more relaxed with each breath, releasing any tensions. Now allow your breathing to go back to normal.

Allow your attention to drift to your hands. Slowly open your eyes and look at your hands. Notice everything about them. Trace around each hand. Feel your hands, look at them. Remember all that they can do--defend you, reach out to meet your needs, touch, express and receive attention, give pleasure, pick up information.

Now decide who will be "I" and who will be "II." Partner "I," take partner "II's" hands in yours. Partner "II" see if you can allow your partner to fully hold your hands as you relax. Partner "I," look at and touch your partner's hands. Experiment with different types of touch--rubbing, stroking, light touches, playful touches, slow, fast. See if you can sense the kinds of touch your partner likes. Partner "II," see if you can communicate, without words, what you like. Try to relax into the experience of being given to, fully supported. Allow yourself some movement. With movement comes aliveness. See if you can give your partner the kind of touch (s)he desires. Keep attuned to your partner's changing wishes.

Now slowly bring this touching experience to a close. Partner "I," begin to say "goodbye" to Partner "II" with your hands. Keep your eyes closed and reflect for a moment on this experience.

Now switch roles. Partner "II," take Partner "I's" hands in yours...and repeat the entire experience.

When you are through, silently reflect on the following. Then write your responses below.

1. What was it like to give and to receive touch?

_____

_____

_____

2. Were you able to communicate without words the touches that you liked?

_____
_____
_____
_____

3. Were you able to sense your partner's wishes?

_____
_____
_____
_____

4. How well are you attuned to each other?

_____
_____
_____
_____

5. How important is touch in your relationship?

_____
_____
_____
_____

6. Has the importance of touch in your relationship changed over time? Explain.

_____
_____
_____
_____

Exercise 12

Boundaries: Values

PURPOSE:

Persons in troubled relationships often have problems developing a clear and independent sense of self. Some learn that another's attempt at intimacy is an invasion of privacy. Others become practically boundariless--they do not know where they end and another begins. These individuals find it difficult to set limits or to say "no."

The purpose of this exercise is to:

- **clarify** one's own value system;

- **find** out what's important to you;

- **identify** shared values;

- **learn** about conflicting values and how they affect the relationship.

TASK:

1. On separate sheets of paper, each partner lists at least five (or more) values they hold dear. Next to each value record the name of the person from whom you learned this value. Then compare values and summarize below:

Values Unique to You	Values Unique to Your Partner	Shared Values
_____	_____	_____
_____	_____	_____
_____	_____	_____
_____	_____	_____
_____	_____	_____

2. Which of the above values, if any, need modification for your relationship to improve? Have you reassessed these values to see if they are working for you?

_____

_____

_____

_____

_____

Body Boundaries

Exercise 13

PURPOSE:

Many couples feel uncomfortable when talking about touch. Because touch can involve sex, it may be an area which becomes confusing and a source of conflict. Many couples have not had healthy role models to demonstrate appropriate and affectionate contact, so some partners avoid touching or even talking about touching. Men often do not differentiate between affectionate touch and touch leading to sex. Women are often reticent about being assertive in this area. Sharing honestly can be scary, but productive, since it can serve as one way to dissolve two myths: touch means sex and sex means intimacy.

TASK:

On separate sheets of paper, partners should write answers about body boundaries listed below, then compare lists.

1. What are the body areas I **always** like to have touched?

_____

_____

2. What are the body areas I **sometimes** like to have touched?

_____

_____

3. What are the body areas I **never** like to have touched?

_____

_____

4. What are the body areas your partner **always** likes to have touched?

_____

_____

5. What are the body areas your partner **sometimes** likes to have touched?

_____

_____

6. What are the body areas your partner **never** likes to have touched?

_____

_____

7. After comparing your lists, how accurate were each of you? Record and discuss.

_____

_____

_____

_____

8. How do you let your partner know how and when you want to be touched?

_____

_____

_____

_____

Exercise 14

Space and Time Boundaries

PURPOSE:

It is important to find out whether you and your partner are satisfied with time and space management in the relationship. As children, some of us had little or no private space. Some of us were told that our rooms or belongings were private--only to find that such spaces were invaded regularly with little or no regard for how we felt. As adults, violations of space may seem perfectly natural to one partner but be absolutely unacceptable to the other partner. It is important for each to determine and express spatial needs so that clear boundaries can be set and honored. Lines need to be drawn so that both partners have space to call their own.

Time is another important issue. Many adults had homes where they had either too much or too little alone time. Some families had unbending rules around time: everyone sat down to dinner every night at a certain hour. Others had few requirements: members fixed their own plates and ate in front of the TV. Partners need to discuss the importance of both alone **and** together time, and to encourage one another to share feelings so that they can reach a healthy balance in the relationship.

TASK:

Answer the following questions and discuss these answers with your partner.

1. What space(s) in your home is personal which **no one else** uses (e.g., study, sewing room, desk area, favorite chair, separate bedroom)?

_____

_____

_____

_____

_____

2. What time(s) do you prefer to spend alone? Do you let your partner know when you need alone time?

_____

_____

3. When does your whole family spend time together?

_____

_____

4. What kinds of activities do you do with your entire family? (For example, do you go to church together as a family? Do you eat certain meals together?)

_____
_____
_____
_____
_____

5. Do you and your spouse set aside times to spend together alone? When? How often?

_____
_____
_____
_____
_____

6. If you have children, do each of you spend individual time with each of your children? How frequently?

_____
_____
_____
_____
_____

7. Are there times when all your children are together without parents or anyone else? How regular are these occasions? What kinds of things do they do together?

_____
_____
_____
_____
_____

8. How much time and emotional energy do you invest in your children's activities?

_____
_____
_____
_____
_____

9. Do you have separate friends with whom you socialize without your partner being present? How often? Do you ever feel jealous or left out when your partner is with his or her friends?

_____
_____
_____
_____
_____

10. Do you invite people into your home? Is there agreement about when and how often this should happen?

_____
_____
_____
_____
_____

11. Do people visit your home uninvited? How often does this happen? How do each of you feel about this?

_____
_____
_____
_____
_____

12. If any of your children have left home, how did your family manage that separation? How much contact do you have with these children now? (Be specific: two times per week, one time per month, twice yearly?)

_____

_____

_____

_____

_____

Exercise 15

Interest Boundaries

PURPOSE:

Many couples from dysfunctional families fall into the trap of fusing their interests and thus lose themselves in the process. Others do almost everything separately and are unwilling to make any compromises or try anything new in the interest of sharing hobbies, sports or other activities. Maintaining interests unique to each, as well as finding common interests, are both important in healthy relationships. This activity helps you to assess your balance of individual and shared interests.

TASK:

On separate sheets of paper, each partner lists six or eight things they like to do--jogging, reading, traveling, etc. Once again, compare lists.

Favorite Personal Activities:

_____

_____

_____

_____

Interests Common to Both of Us:

_____

_____

_____

_____

1. How many interests do you share? _____

2. Have your common interests increased or decreased since you first met? Why?

_____

_____

_____

_____

_____

3. Would either or both of you like to develop more **common** or **different** interests? If so, how could that happen?

_____
_____
_____
_____

4. How could having more common or more unique activities affect your relationship?

_____
_____
_____
_____
_____

Exercise 16

Differences

PURPOSE:

In the disillusionment stage of relationships, partners are aware of their deep differences. These differences can be a source of conflict and they are reminders that the partner is not an extension of self but is a separate human being. This activity helps couples to identify and acknowledge basic differences, as well as to begin to see their differences as strengths.

TASK:

Take a moment to list on a separate sheet of paper some of the important differences between you and your partner. When you are finished, compare your list with your partner's list.

Differences	I Am:	My Partner Is:
Physical	_____	_____
	_____	_____
	_____	_____
	_____	_____
Personality or temperament	_____	_____
	_____	_____
	_____	_____
	_____	_____
Educational background	_____	_____
	_____	_____
	_____	_____
	_____	_____
Abilities	_____	_____
	_____	_____
	_____	_____
	_____	_____

Differences	I Am:	My Partner Is:
Interests	_____	_____
	_____	_____
	_____	_____
	_____	_____
Habits (early morning/late night person, orderly/ disorganized; TV; climate, preferences, etc.)	_____	_____
	_____	_____
	_____	_____
	_____	_____
Expectations and opinions (role of men and women, religious or political convictions, etc.)	_____	_____
	_____	_____
	_____	_____
	_____	_____
Values	_____	_____
	_____	_____
	_____	_____
	_____	_____
Tempo	_____	_____
	_____	_____
	_____	_____
	_____	_____

1. Which differences do you most appreciate in your partner?

_____

_____

_____

_____

2. Which differences do you see as problems?

_____
_____
_____
_____
_____

3. How do you manage these differences?

_____
_____
_____
_____
_____

4. What are the similarities and differences between you and your partner in how you manage differences, and how your **parents** managed their differences?

Similarities	Differences
_____	_____
_____	_____
_____	_____
_____	_____
_____	_____

Exercise 17

Blaming and Defending

PURPOSE:

Even though it is damaging to the relationship, partners often are critical of each other without even realizing it. This exercise helps partners to recognize this pattern.

TASK:

Go through each of the following steps with your partner. Then discuss your experience and write down what you have gained from the exercise.

1. Silently look at your partner and think all the ways you find fault with him or her:

    Examples:

    "You always do..."

    "You can be so..."

    "You never..."

    _____
    _____
    _____
    _____
    _____

2. Communicate each of these blaming statements to your partner and give examples to illustrate your observations.

    _____
    _____
    _____
    _____
    _____

3. Now reverse the process. Have your partner deliver blaming statements to you.

_____
_____
_____
_____
_____

4. Now try replacing each blaming statement with a statement about how you feel about the other's behavior.

Example:

Blaming: You never put anything away after you use it.

"I"-statement: I feel frustrated when you don't put the tools away. They create clutter and I have trouble finding them."

_____
_____
_____
_____
_____

5. Now, rather than defending yourself, take one or two statements from your partner's list and assume responsibility for your actions.

Example:

"Yes, I do tend to create clutter. I will try to do a better job of picking up after myself."

_____
_____
_____
_____
_____

Exercise 18

The Stress Ballet*

PURPOSE:

This exercise will help partners to heighten their awareness of how they **communicate under stress.** Through such awareness you can increase your ability to make certain **choices rather than** continuing to behave in habitual ways.

TASK:

1. Each partner privately chooses one of the following communication stances:

Placater

    Words: ingratiating, apologizing, never disagreeing, "whatever you say..."
    Body: whiny voice, body slumped, cowering, submissive
    Insides: feels worthless, helpless

Blamer

    Words: critical, put-downs, "You always," You never," tyrannical
    Body: tight muscles, blood pressure increasing, flushing, voice tense and often loud, breathing restricted
    Insides: lonely, scared

Super-Reasonable

    Words: very reasonable, logical, no feeling shows, abstract, dry, superior, calm, cool
    Body: rigid, little expressiveness, voice monotone, little movement
    Insides: vulnerable

Irrelevant

    Words: distracting, makes no sense
    Body: ungrounded, uncoordinated, voice singsong or incongruent with the words, lots of movement
    Insides: purposeless, feels there's no place for me, dizzy, unfocused

Note: These stances represent how each is trying to preserve his or her self-worth. We tend to adopt these roles when under stress.

2. Plan something together (for example, a vacation) or discuss a small issue, using a chosen stance.

---

*Adapted from Satir, Virginia. *The New Peoplemaking*. Science and Behavior Books, Inc.: Mountain View, CA, 1988.

3. Stop action after 3-4 minutes.

   a. Notice what you are feeling (emotionally, physically)
   b. Do you feel loved? Valued?
   c. Does life seem hopeful?

4. Each person privately chooses another role. Repeat procedure until each partner has had an opportunity to practice each stance.

5. Discuss:

   a. Which stance(s) seem(s) most familiar to you?

   _____
   _____
   _____

   b. What stance(s) would characterize each of your parents?

   _____
   _____
   _____

   c. What internal resources do you think you would need in order to relate to each other more positively?

   _____
   _____
   _____

   d. How can you help yourself and each other recognize when you are in these stress stances?

   _____
   _____
   _____

Exercise 19

Toy Defense[*]

PURPOSE:

This exercise heightens one's awareness of personal defensive styles. It will help partners to react differently to each other. The goal is to break up the defensive interactions in which partners often get lost. This activity tunes partners into their own and their partner's typical defensive style. The playfulness of the activity is enormously helpful in coping with and breaking through habitual, painful interactive styles.

TASK:

1. What is your favorite defense?

    For example:

    blaming   controlling
    distracting   placating
    intellectualizing   withdrawing

Partner I _____ Partner II _____

2. Use your imagination and create a toy which incorporates your favorite defensive mode.

    Example:

    "Tilly the Tank"
    "The Control Doll House"
    "The Disappearing Mask"
    "Bernice the Blaster"

Partner I _____ Partner II _____

3. Create an advertisement for your toy. Record below and include the following:

    - Describe what it does
    - What is its function: How does it protect you?
    - What is its value? Why should everyone have one?
    - What does it cost?

---

[*]Based on Bunny Duhl's "Toy Exercise" presented at the Boston Family Institute, Boston, MA, 1974.

Example:

Presenting the Perfect Control Dollhouse!!!

This exact replica of your home, complete with family members in miniature, is now yours to command. You decide where they go, how they dress, what they say. From the outside, it will always look like you have a perfect family.

You'll feel like you're in perfect control with the Perfect Control Dollhouse!!!

Partner I

_____
_____
_____
_____

Partner II

_____
_____
_____
_____

(Writing the advertisement helps create psychological distance from your defense so that you can better work with it.)

4. Act out your toy. Interact with your partner's toy. How does it fit with your partner's toy? If in a group, try your toy out with others. Does your toy get along better with another's toy? Interact again with your partner's toy. Now try on your partner's toy.

(Note: There's nothing right or wrong about our toy but sometimes it doesn't interact very well with our partner's defensive style.)

5. Does your toy work for you? How? In what contexts? What are its psychological costs? What are the relationship costs?

Partner I

_____
_____
_____
_____

Partner II

_____
_____
_____
_____

6. Do you need to invent a new protection? **What one? Invent a new toy** and surprise your partner with it.

Partner I

_____
_____
_____
_____

Partner II

_____
_____
_____
_____

Part D
STRENGTHS

People need a four to one praise/criticism ratio in order to develop and maintain high self-esteem (Carlock and Frey, 1989). Couples, too, need to recognize positive qualities in each other in order to feel good about their relationship. Yet, for many couples regular praising of each other is often lacking. Such adults were seldom praised as they were growing up and so are not trained to acknowledge the positive qualities in themselves or their relationships. In the therapy setting, particularly, couples often describe problems in their relationships, but hesitate when asked about their strengths.

Appreciation of each other's assets forms a solid foundation for couples to build on and helps them to keep things in perspective when times are tough. The following activities give partners a chance to renew and reinvest in external sources of support and to acknowledge their inner resources.

Exercise 20

Wheel of Support*

PURPOSE:

This exercise will help you identify sources of support.

TASK:

Draw a wheel of support to depict those people in your life who currently enhance your sense of "couple-hood." Place your names in a circle in the middle of a sheet of paper. Surround that circle with other circles representing people who support your relationship. These people could be other couples, siblings, parents, in-laws, single friends, neighbors, a therapist, a minister or a doctor. (If you are in a 12-step program you might draw two wheels of support, one before recovery and one after moving into recovery and compare the two or, you may draw a Wheel of Support for each phase of your relationship.)

Near each of the circles use a word or phrase to describe what it is they give to your relationship. Draw heavy lines to those who support you most; thin lines to those who support is there, but not as strong (see illustration).

When you complete the **Wheel of Support,** discuss the following with your partner:

1. Are you satisfied with the amount of support you see depicted, or do either or both of you see the need to expand your relationship support system? How could that happen?

_____

_____

_____

2. Did either of you disagree on who is supportive and who is not?

_____

_____

_____

3. Do you value and use your support system?

_____

_____

_____

---

*Adapted from Virginia Satir and J. Banmen. VERBATIM: *Virginia Satir Process Community III.* Delta Psychological Associates, Inc., 11213 Canyon Crescent, N. Delta, B.C., Canada, 1983.

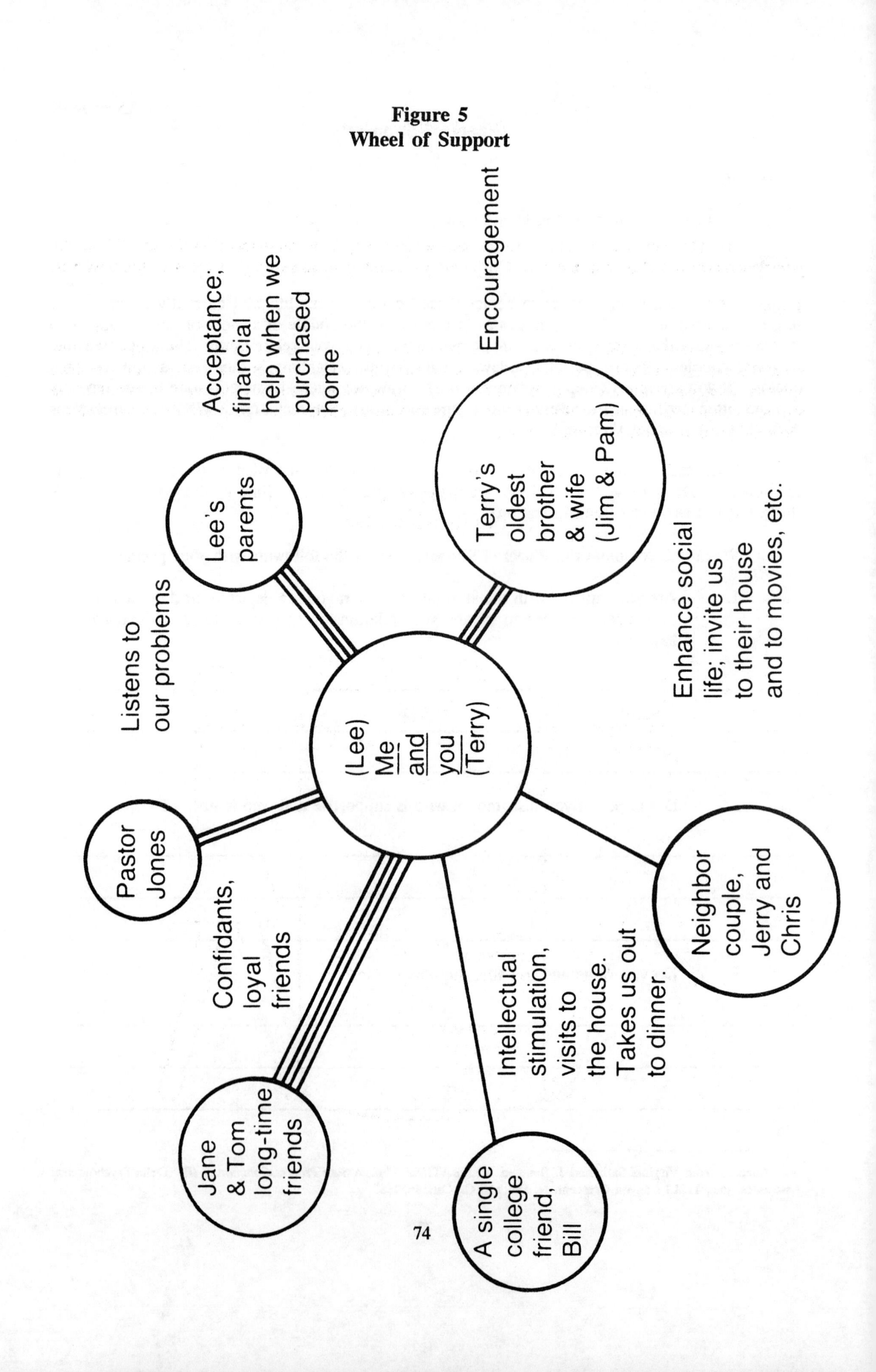

Figure 5
Wheel of Support

Exercise 21

Relationship Glue

PURPOSE:

Troubled couples find it helpful to review the strengths in their relationship, identifying the glue which cements their partnership. This activity requests that you shift your focus to the positives.

TASK:

On a separate sheet of paper, place the items which you see as "couple strengths." A few examples are listed below. Consider the following major life areas: domestic, social, mental, physical, spiritual, financial, sexual, vocational, child rearing. By recalling qualities which help to "weather the storms," couples can identify resources and affirm common beliefs, values, and behaviors which form the solid ground helpful in future crises.

Figure 6
Relationship Glue

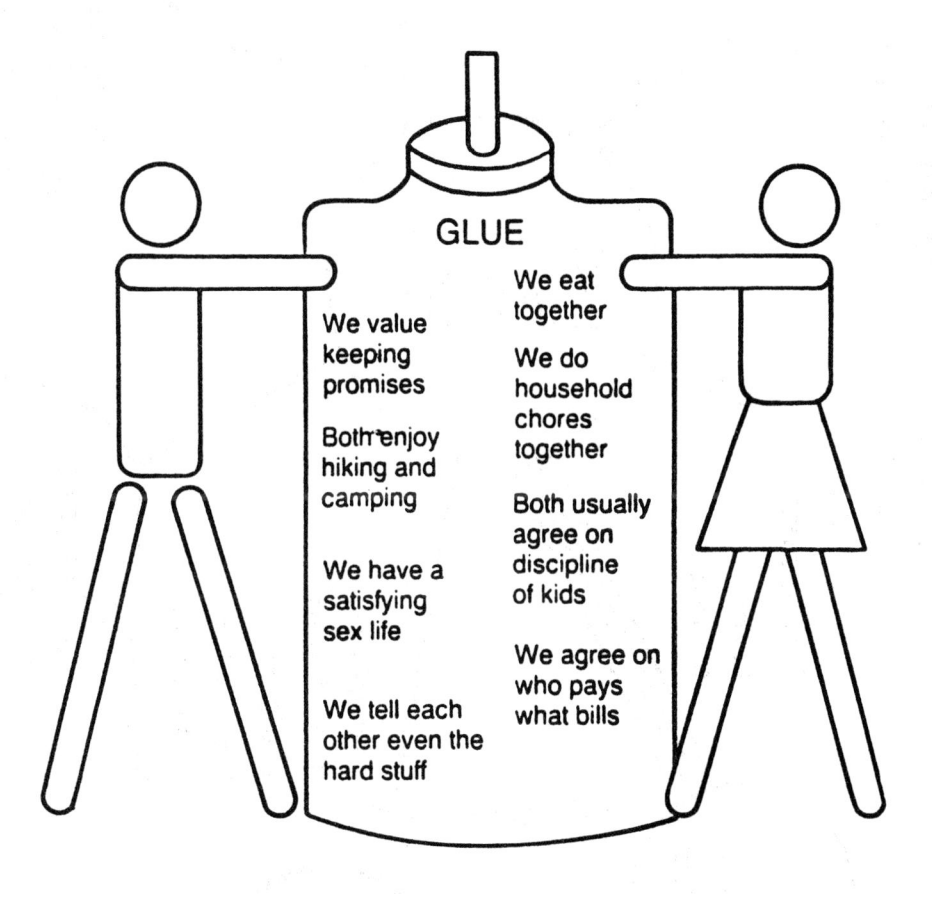

GLUE

- We value keeping promises
- Both enjoy hiking and camping
- We have a satisfying sex life
- We tell each other even the hard stuff
- We eat together
- We do household chores together
- Both usually agree on discipline of kids
- We agree on who pays what bills

Exercise 22

Famous Figures*

PURPOSE:

Often we are not aware of many of our inner resources. This is particularly true of couples in crisis. By being more in touch with our strengths, we can better handle conflicts and problems which arise in our relationship.

TASK:

Each partner lists the name of five **famous** people whom he or she admires (fictional or real, from politics, history, science, cartoons, films, novels, anthropology, religion, etc.). Next to each name write the quality you associate with the person.

Example:

Kathryn Hepburn   feisty, independent

Partner I: Famous Person	Quality	Partner II: Famous Person	Quality
1.		1.	
2.		2.	
3.		3.	
4.		4.	
5.		5.	

Look over each of the characteristics you listed. How is each quality (if any) you listed true for you? Think of a time when you displayed that characteristic or look for ways the quality fits you now. If you have trouble owning a particular trait, ask your partner to help you see if that quality is true for you now, or could be true for you with help.

Partner I:
_____
_____

Partner II:
_____
_____

---

*Adapted from V. Satir and J. Banmen. VERBATIM: *Virginia Satir Process Community III*. 11213 Canyon Crescent, N. Delta, B.C., Canada. 1983.

Exercise 23

Sharing Your Love

PURPOSE:

After the initial glow has dimmed in relationships, partners frequently take each other for granted. They neglect those ways they demonstrated their love during the romantic stage. In this exercise we ask that you restore some of these thoughtful demonstrations of love.

TASK:

1. Write down three times when your partner expressed love to you when you didn't expect it.

Partner I:

1. _____
2. _____
3. _____

Partner II:

1. _____
2. _____
3. _____

2. Now think of some way you could surprise your partner tomorrow with an expression of your love. Write down what you could do. Do this privately so that it can be a surprise.

NOW DO IT!

3. From your perspective write about the effect of the previous expressions of love shown by you and your partner.

On Me	**On my Partner**
_____	_____
_____	_____
_____	_____
_____	_____
_____	_____

4. Have your partner write down, from his or her perspective, the effect of the above expressions of love:

    On Me   **On my Partner**

_____   _____

_____   _____

_____   _____

_____   _____

_____   _____

Exercise 24
What I Like About You and Me*

PURPOSE:

This exercise is designed to counteract that "inner critic" and to replace it with a wise and accepting person who sends positive messages to self and to your partner.

Virginia Satir (1978) developed the self-mandala (graphically depicted as a series of concentric circles) which represents a whole person. She includes eight essential levels or "selves" which interact with the "I" or personal self:

1. Physical - body, breathing, exercise

2. Nutritional - what is ingested (food and drink)

3. Sensual - sights, sounds, tastes, smells, touch, movement

4. Emotional - the self which experiences feelings

5. Intellectual - thoughts, facts

6. Interactional - social self

7. Contextual - environmental factors such as time, space, light, air, sound, color

8. Spiritual - one's relationship to a universal life force

TASK:

On the lines below, each partner writes something positive about each of the following aspects of self and partner. Then share the positive messages with one another.

Partner I:

Me	My Partner
Physical: (Example: I like the way I'm exercising my body 3x per week.)	(You have great muscle tone.)

_____

_____

_____

*Adapted from *Your Many Faces* by Virginia Satir, Millbrae, CA: Celestial Arts. 1978.

b. Nutritional

_____
_____
_____

c. Sensual

_____
_____
_____

d. Emotional

_____
_____
_____

e. Intellectual

_____
_____
_____

f. Interactional

_____
_____
_____

g. Contextual

_____
_____
_____

h.   Spiritual

_____
_____
_____

After sharing your responses to the preceeding items, respond to the following:

1.   Was it difficult to compliment yourself? Your partner?

_____
_____
_____

2.   Did the "inner critic" or blamer emerge as you worked?

_____
_____
_____

3.   Share with your partner what pleased or surprised you most about the "likes."

_____
_____
_____

Part E
MAINTAINING OUR RELATIONSHIP

> "the main cry seems to be for greater feelings of individual self-esteem and loving, nurturing contexts that go with it." (Satir 1988)

The next few exercises are designed to maintain and improve the health of a couple's relationship. We have found them to be quite helpful. Taking the emotional temperature of your partnership, learning to ask for what you want, sharing updated hopes and dreams, and scheduling playtime (whether used as directed or tailored to fit your needs) will move you toward becoming a better functioning couple.

Exercise 25

Taking the Temperature of the Relationship*

PURPOSE:

This exercise can help you and your partner keep current with each other. It is a good relationship maintenance activity.

TASK:

Sit down with your partner and share thoughts and feelings about any or all of the following categories. Do this weekly (see illustration).

Appreciations

1.	What did each of you appreciate about your partner this week?	Example: "I appreciated the fact that you listened to my anxiety about the job interview."
2.	What did each of you like about the way you interacted **as a couple**?	Example: "Hooray! We compromised."

In a healthy relationship, appreciations outnumber criticisms by about four to one.

Irritations/Recommendations for Change

1.	Is there anything you did **not** like about the way we interacted?	Example: "We stopped before we reached a solution acceptable to both of us. Let's make a commitment to "hang in there" next time."
2.	How could we interact differently in the future?	Example: "You've been away a lot lately. I'm wondering if we could set aside some time this coming weekend just to talk and play."

Worries/Concerns

1.	Let your partner know of any internal or external concerns.	Example: "I'm no longer satisfied with the pediatrician. I'm wondering if you would support a change.
2.	Ask for any comfort, support you would like.	Example: "I'm feeling scared. Will you hold me?"

---

*Adapted from Satir & Banmen. VERBATIM: *Virginia Satir Process Community III*. N. Delta, B.C., Canada: Delta Psychological Associates, Inc., 1983.

New Information Needed/Offered

1. Offer information that affects both partners.

   Example: "I found a babysitter for the office party."

2. Check out/clarify current or upcoming dates, purchases, plans.

   Example: "Would you give me your out of town schedule for the next three months so we can coordinate time together."

Wishes/Dreams
(Short term and long range)

1. Each partner expresses hopes and dreams.

   Example: "The Joffrey Ballet is coming to town. I'd love to go."

2. Add any suggestions you have to help make your dreams come true.

   Example: "I'd like to go to the Bahamas with you next year or the year after. Do you think we could save $100 a month for that purpose?"

Note: Be aware of whether or not you consistently skip over certain categories. For instance, if you tend to avoid the irritations/recommendations section, you might need to take a look at your ability to express anger. If you avoid sharing appreciations, review your ability to express affection.

**Figure 7
TEMPERATURE READING**

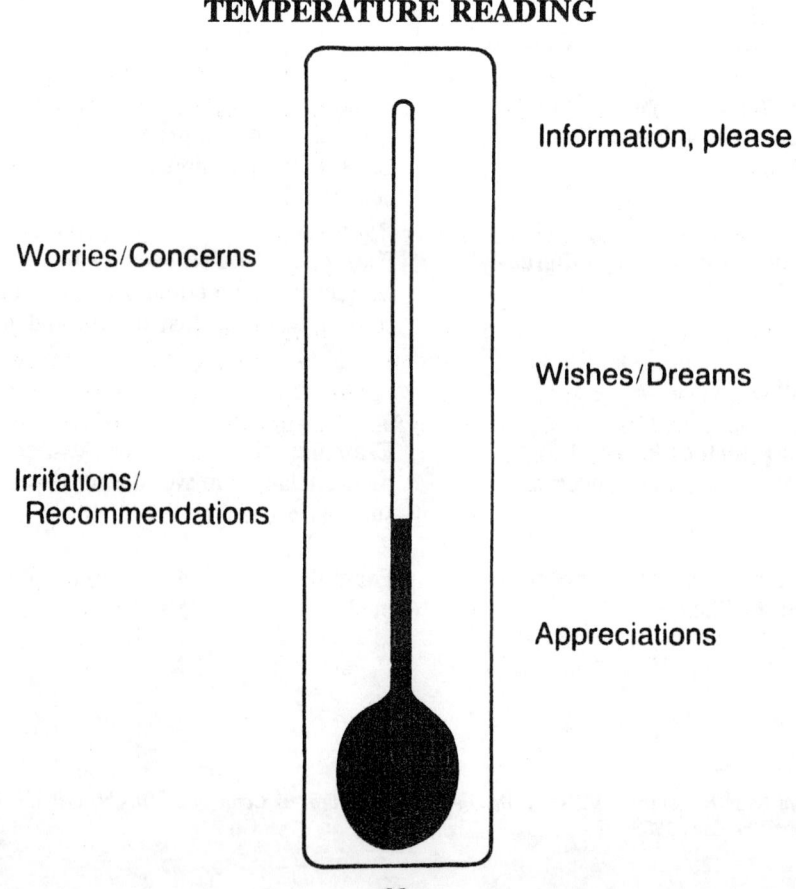

Exercise 26

Connect-O-Meter

PURPOSE:

This exercise is designed for couples who tend towards disengagement; that is, excessive and prolonged distancing from each other. It will help couples interrupt distancing patterns by requiring a daily monitoring of their experience of the closeness/distance dimension of their relationship.

TASK:

1. Each couple selects a unique refrigerator magnet to represent him or herself. The magnets are then placed at a distance that represents the partner's perceived closeness at the moment.

2. Daily, each partner adjusts his or her magnet to represent the degree of closeness experienced.

3. Each partner must also agree to comment daily on his or her own and partner's adjustments.

    For example: "I noticed you moved your magnet far away from mine. What is this in response to? Let's talk about how we can bridge the distance."

    or

    "I moved my magnet away from yours. I don't think we've been spending enough time together lately. Let's go for a walk and talk."

    or

    "I moved my magnet closer to yours this afternoon. Listening to you talk about memories of your father made me feel really close to you."

Not only should partners comment on what's happening between them, they should also talk about what the increased distance or closeness is in response to. In the case of unwanted distance, offer suggestions about how to bridge the gap. There are, of course, times when distance is wanted and can be a healthy part of relationships. Habitual and prolonged distance, however, can damage a relationship if left unattended.

Exercise 27

Getting Your Needs Met

PURPOSE:

In successful relationships, partners have the ability to open their senses--to see and hear and ask for what they want. This exercise will help couples to better meet mutual needs.

TASKS:

1. In the spaces provided below, write a list of needs, wants and wishes that you would like your partner to meet. Also list what you think are the needs, wants and wishes of your partner. Be sure to be clear and specific. For instance, don't ask for love and support. Rather, ask specifically for what your partner could do or say to give you this feeling. (Asking does not guarantee that you will get what you want, but if you ask, you definitely increase your chances.)

Self	**Partner**
I need	My partner needs
_____	_____
_____	_____
_____	_____
_____	_____
I want	My partner wants
_____	_____
_____	_____
_____	_____
_____	_____
I would like	My partner would like
_____	_____
_____	_____
_____	_____
_____	_____

2. Ask your partner to then write down what she thinks I need, want and like; and what she or he needs, wants and would like.

_____
_____
_____
_____
_____

3. Each partner should now select a need of the other and contract to fill this need within a specified period of time. Write your contracts below:

   a. Your contract

   _____
   _____
   _____
   _____
   _____

   b. Your partner's contract

   _____
   _____
   _____
   _____
   _____

4. After completing the contracts, write about your reactions.

_____
_____
_____
_____
_____

Exercise 28

Make a Wish

PURPOSE:

It could be said that without hope we die, without dreams we can't move forward. When we verbalize a wish or a dream, we take the first step towards actualizing that picture in our lives.

TASK:

Pretend that you have the power to make a wish come true. On a sheet of paper, describe changes you would like in your relationship.

Examples:

- Play more together.

- Plan and carry out a project.

- Spend 1/2 hour cuddling and talking each day.

Now share your wishes with one another. To actualize the wish you described, each partner will need to make some changes. Note the following:

Changes I would need to make	Changes my partner would need to make
_____	_____
_____	_____
_____	_____
_____	_____
_____	_____

1. Discuss each of the changes you desire. Pick one from your partner's list to work on.

_____
_____
_____
_____
_____

2. Compliment each other when you notice that your partner tries to help fulfill your wishes.

3. Once a week evaluate how successful you've been in putting your wishes into action. What did each of you contribute to your successes?

Exercise 29
Intimacy Request

PURPOSE:

Learning to ask for what you want, and learning to be specific with this request, circumvents problems which arise from expectations to "mind-read." You have a much better chance of getting what you want if you learn to ask. In this activity, **both** partners make a request and have it fulfilled so that the experience will be mutual.

TASK:

Each partner agrees to complete a 15 minute intimacy request of their partner in the course of a morning, afternoon, or evening together. The request is **not** to include sexual activities, but rather emotional or nurturing activities.

Examples:
- back rub
- foot rub
- listen to me without trying to problem solve
- take a bath together
- cuddle in bed together
- tell me what you appreciate about me

Discuss your feeling reactions to the experience. Contract for future exchange sessions.

Exercise 30

Monthly Mystery

PURPOSE:

It is wise to schedule some play time in our lives. This activity calls for one person to initiate and plan a special day of fun while the other person co-operates by trusting and being spontaneous. An element of surprise supplies an "outlandish air"--an antidote to rigidity and control.

TASK:

Partners decide on one day per month which will be set aside as "Mystery play day." Partners take turns planning the day. Whoever is the planner tells the other:

- the time to be ready;
- what type of clothing is suitable;
- about how long they'll be engaged; and
- if a babysitter is needed.

The other partner agrees to:

- be ready on time;
- dress properly;
- be a cooperative playmate.

This is a great way to get to do some of the things you've been putting off and to enjoy new places and new experiences as a couple. Be creative: art fairs, kite-flying, canoe trips, hiking, concerts, picnics, train or boat rides are a few ideas. This gives you a chance to be good to that "little kid" inside. Have fun!

After each event, discuss and record answers to the following:

1. What went well?

_____

_____

_____

_____

2. What (if anything) was problematic?

_____
_____
_____
_____

3. What creative ideas do or did you have to manage that which is problematic?

_____
_____
_____
_____

BIBLIOGRAPHY

Anderson, C. and Malloy, E. "Family photographs: in treatment and training," *Family Process 15*, 259-264.

Campbell, S. *The Couple's Journey: Intimacy as a Path to Wholeness*. San Luis Obispo, CA: Impact Publishers, 1980.

Carlock, J. and Frey, D. *Enhancing Self-esteem*. Muncie, IN: Accelerated Development, 1989.

Duhl, B. *Toy Exercise* presented at the Boston Family Institute, Boston, MA, 1974.

Duhl, B. *The Interpersonal Vulnerability Contract* presented at the First Family Encounter, Mexico, City, Mexico, November 1976.

Frew, J. "Clarity of Boundary Conditions in Interpersonal Context." *The Gestalt Journal*, Vol. 6, No. 2, 117-123.

Hendricks, G. and Hendricks, K. *Centering and the Art of Intimacy*. New York, NY: Brunner/Mazel, 1987.

Kramer, J.R. *Family Interfaces: Transgenerational Patterns*. New York: Bruner/Mazel, 1985.

Napier, A. and Whitaker, C. *The Family Crucible*. New York, NY: Harper and Row, 1978.

Polster, I. and Polster, M. *Gestalt Therapy Integrated*. New York, NY: Vintage Books, Random House, 1973.

Satir, V. *Your Many Faces*. Millbrae, CA: Celestial Arts, 1978.

Satir, V. and Baldwin, M. *Satir Step by Step, a Guide to Creating Change in Families*. Palo Alto, CA: Science and Behavior Books, 1983.

Satir, V. and Banmen, J. *Virginia Satir VERBATIM: Process Community III*. N. Delta, B.C., Canada: Delta Psychological Associates, Inc., 1983.

Satir, V. *Conjoint Family Therapy*. Palo Alto, CA: Science and Bahvior Books, 1983.

Satir, V. *The New Peoplemaking*. Mountain View, CA: Science and Behavior Books, 1988.

Scarf, M. *Intimate Partners*. New York: Random House, 1987.

Schwartz, R. and Schwartz, L. *Becoming a Couple, Making the Most of Every Stage of Your Relationship*. Englewood Cliffs, New Jersey: Prentice-Hall, Inc, 1980.

Zinker, J. and Nevis, S. *The Gestalt Theory of Couple and Family Interactions*. Cleveland, OH: Gestalt Institute of Cleveland, 1981.